BUILD YOUR OWN BOATS

Thanks to the creative team:
Senior Editor: Alice Peebles
Fact checking: Tom Jackson
Design: Perfect Bound Ltd

Original edition copyright 2017 by Hungry Tomato Ltd.
Copyright © 2018 by Lerner Publishing Group, Inc.

Hungry Tomato® is a trademark of Lerner Publishing Group, Inc.

Hungry Tomato®
A division of Lerner Publishing Group, Inc.
241 First Avenue North
Minneapolis, MN 55401 USA

For reading levels and more information, look up
this title at www.lernerbooks.com.

Main body text set in Neutraliser Serif Regular 9.75/13.

Library of Congress Cataloging-in-Publication Data

The Cataloging-in-Publication Data for *Build Your Own Boats* is
on file at the Library of Congress.
ISBN 978-1-5124-5969-2 (lib. bdg.)
ISBN 978-1-5124-9871-4 (EB pdf)

Manufactured in the United States of America
1-43028-27697-9/13/2017

MAKERSPACE MODELS
BUILD YOUR OWN BOATS

BY ROB IVES

HUNGRY TOMATO®
Minneapolis

SAFETY FIRST

Take care and use good sense when making these fun model boats. They are all straightforward, but some activities call for cutting materials, drilling holes, and other skills for which you should ask an adult assistant for help (see below).

Every project includes a list of supplies that you will need. Most will be stuff that you can find around the house or buy inexpensively online or at a local hardware store.

We have included "How It Works" for each model, to explain in simple terms the engineering or scientific principles that make the model move. And for some, there is a "Real-World Engineering" snippet that tells you more about actual watercraft (or water creatures!).

You may want to try the models out at a local pond or swimming pool—just make sure you take an adult to act as first mate. Even the captain hands over the wheel sometimes!

Watch out for this sign accompanying some model instructions. You may need help from an adult with completing these tasks.

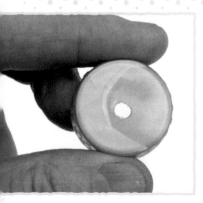

CONTENTS

WATER VEHICLES   6

COOL CATAMARAN   8

JETTIN' ALONG   12

PADDLE POWER   14

WATER BUG   16

SAIL AWAY   20

DEEP DIVER   22

SWAMP BOAT   26

GLOSSARY   30

INDEX   32

WATER VEHICLES

It's often said that there's nothing half as nice as messing about in boats or with boats—whether you go anywhere or not.

Now you can build eight amazing watercraft models and go on trips to the ocean deep—or maybe just to the local pond or swimming pool (having trained up a trusty adult crew, of course). Or just try them out in your bath or inflatable backyard pool!

Climb aboard a tin-can catamaran or cruise in a paddle boat—driven just by rubber band energy. Add a motor to a leggy water bug or a flat-bottomed swamp boat for extra zoom. Or just watch the breeze fill the sail on your raft and see your sub slowly sink down, down, down, then forge silently ahead, powered by a propeller, like the real thing.

So get your tools and materials together, start building, and see how these boats move—and compare them to find out which is fastest and floatiest . . .

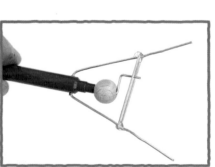

TOP TIPS

* Before you start on any of the models, read the step-by-step instructions all the way through to get an idea of what you're aiming for. The pictures show what the steps tell you to do.

* A project may need pencils to be cut into sections. Ask an adult for help with this and use a cutting board or similar surface to cut on. An efficient way to do it is to cut each face of the pencil in turn with a utility knife, then snap it apart. Tidy up any unevenness with the knife.

TOOL KIT

- Ruler
- Utility knife
- Gaffer tape (or duct tape)
- Clear tape
- Tape measure
- Needle-nose pliers
- Kitchen scissors
- Tracing paper
- Wire cutters
- White glue
- Epoxy glue
- Super glue
- Hot glue gun
- Craft drill

EPOXY

WHITE GLUE

SUPER GLUE

COOL CATAMARAN

The "cat" dates back to ancient Polynesia. Its lightness and stability have kept it very much in use—for fun, sport, and naval operations.

TOOLS:
- Needle-nose pliers
- Tape measure
- Wire cutters
- Gaffer tape (or duct tape)
- Kitchen scissors

YOU WILL NEED:

Large paper clip

0.4–0.5 in. (10–12 mm) wooden bead

Stiff 0.08 in. (2 mm) garden wire

Two 5 in. x 2 in. (130 x 50 mm) energy drink cans

Large rubber band

Plastic propeller, 5 in. (120 mm) long

Wooden chopstick

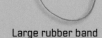

Zip ties

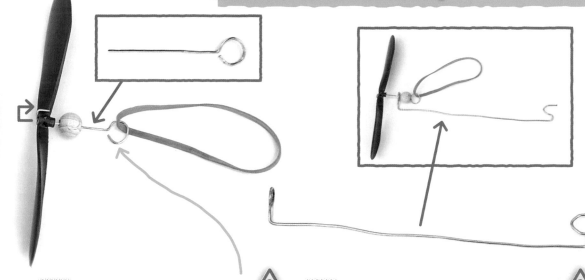

1 Use pliers to straighten the paper clip and make a loop at one end. Thread on the bead, then the propeller, and turn the wire end into a hook. Insert the rubber band in the loop.

2 Cut a 6.3-in. (160 mm) length of garden wire. Use pliers to form a loop at one end and a hook at the other, as in the picture. This is the propeller wire and will attach to the other section as shown, but don't attach it yet.

3 Cut two pieces of stiff wire, 10 in. (260 mm) long. Form them into two pairs of legs, bent as shown, with a 1-in. (25 mm) loop. Bend the "foot" ends inward.

4 Tape the leg loops to the chopstick with gaffer tape. Tape the propeller wire to the other side of the chopstick. Position the two cans so the drink holes are facing up. Tape the wire feet to the cans to secure the propeller wire loop in place.

5 Fit the propeller section in place as shown. Fix on with zip ties at each end for extra security and trim away the excess with scissors. Wind up the propeller clockwise from the front. Place the catamaran on water, release the propeller and . . .

. . . watch it go!

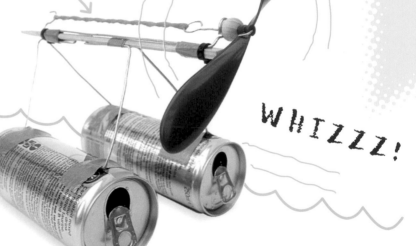

WHIZZZ!

HOW IT WORKS

The model uses an **air propeller** to drive it forward. Air is forced backward using the energy stored in the wound-up rubber band, and this drives the model forward. It's a simple example of Newton's Third Law of Motion: every push one way produces an equal push the opposite way.

REAL-WORLD ENGINEERING

Catamarans are very fast. The **hull** (bottom) is narrow to reduce contact with water so there is less friction to slow them down. The double hull also makes catamarans very stable. This means that the sail will not only stay up in strong winds but can be larger than in single-hulled boats to catch more wind.

SWISHY FISH

The fins have it! They're designed for speed, sudden turns, braking, and keeping upright—probably the best bit of marine engineering ever.

TOOLS:
- Craft drill
- Needle-nose pliers
- Ruler
- Utility knife
- Hot glue gun
- Wire cutters
- Kitchen scissors

YOU WILL NEED:

Toothpick

Four long paper clips

Water-soluble marker

Polystyrene sheet scraps

Soft DVD case

0.5-in. (12 mm) wooden bead

Two pennies

Long rubber band

1 Pull the felt, the end, and the tip out of the pen, leaving the plastic tube. Drill a small hole right through the tube 0.4 in. (10 mm) from the tip with a craft drill.

2 Straighten out a paper clip with pliers. Bend the end over to trap the rubber band.

4 Thread the bead on the wire, then form a dogleg to keep it in place.

3 Cut 1.2 in. (30 mm) off the cocktail stick. Thread the wire through the pen and out of the tip. Slip the stick through the end of the rubber band.

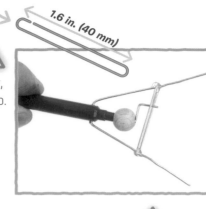

6 Make a thin wire loop, 1.6 in. (40 mm) long, from another paper clip. Fix it to the tail wires using a hot glue gun, with the dogleg inside the slot. Trim the end of the dogleg with wire cutters.

1.6 in. (40 mm)

5 Straighten another paper clip, thread it through the two holes on the pen, and bend it as shown. This will be part of the fish tail.

7 Use kitchen scissors to cut and shape two identical lower body pieces from the DVD case, 3 in. x 1 in. (85 mm x 25 mm) at the widest point across. Glue the pennies to the inside of both pieces.

8 Measure the ends of the tail wires and the distance between them. Cut a curved piece of plastic from the DVD case to fit. Glue it in place.

9 Use a utility knife to cut a 4 in. x 1.4 in. (100 mm x 35 mm) piece of polystyrene for the upper body. Shape it as shown. Glue the body parts to the pen tube and allow to dry. Wind up the rubber band from the cocktail stick end.

Pop the fish in water and watch it swim!

SWISSH!

HOW IT WORKS

As the fish tail flaps from side to side, it sheds tiny vortices from the back, and these move the fish forward. A vortex is a small whirlpool, or a fast-spinning area of water. Paddling a canoe also creates vortices.

REAL-WORLD ENGINEERING

Some fish are speedier than others. The tail fin gives propulsion (forward movement), and deepsea fish with a streamlined body and crescent-shaped tail fin are superfast. Horizontal fins on their sides keep them from rolling as they move along.

JETTIN' ALONG

The jet boat was invented by a New Zealand farmer to be used for navigating shallow rivers. It's a high-speed craft propelled by a pressurized jet of water—but yours is moved by a special fizzy mix!

TOOLS:
- Kitchen scissors
- Epoxy glue
- Clear tape

YOU WILL NEED:

Vinegar

ORIGINAL BAKING SODA

Keeps your home spick and span!

500g ℮

Baking soda

Small plastic soda bottle

Straw with flexible end

. . . and an 8.5 x 11 sheet of paper

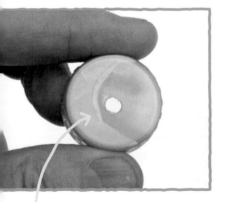

1 Use the point of the scissors to drill a hole in the lid of the bottle to take the straw.

2 Fit the straw in position just below the joint and attach it with Epoxy glue.

3 Pour vinegar into the bottle to a depth of about 0.8 in. (20 mm).

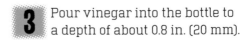

4 Make a cone from the paper, leaving an opening to fit inside the neck of the bottle. Secure with clear tape inside the bottle and trim the top if you wish.

5 Add a heaping teaspoon of baking soda to the vinegar.

6 Quickly screw on the lid—the solution in the bottle will soon bubble and fizz.

Transfer your boat to the water and watch it go with . . . jet power!

FFSSSHHH!

HOW IT WORKS

Pressurized foam from the vinegar–baking soda mixture is forced out through the straw of the jet boat. This creates a **thrust** backward that moves the boat forward over the water.

REAL-WORLD ENGINEERING

Jet boats have a unit inside the stern (rear) that sucks up water, then pumps it out forcefully through a nozzle to push the boat along. They are speedy and have a shallow **draft** (portion of the hull that sits below the water) so are versatile and often used for fun rides.

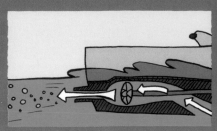

PADDLE POWER

In ancient times, boats powered by paddle wheels, rather than by oars or by sails, were used in places from Europe to China. The first paddle wheels were powered by animals or humans—but all YOU need is a rubber band!

TOOLS:
- Utility knife
- Ruler
- White glue
- Kitchen scissors

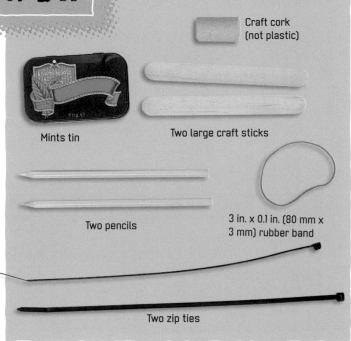

Craft cork (not plastic)

Mints tin

Two large craft sticks

Two pencils

3 in. x 0.1 in. (80 mm x 3 mm) rubber band

Two zip ties

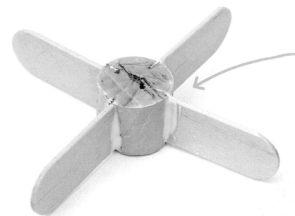

1 Cut the cork in half with a utility knife. Cut four evenly spaced slots in the side of one half. Make them about 0.3 in. (7 mm) deep. Cut four 1.6-in. (40 mm) lengths from the craft sticks, keeping the curved ends. Glue them into the slots in the cork with the white glue.

2 Cut the points off two pencils with a utility knife. To do this, make a nick all the way around, then snap off the end.

3 Tie the pencils to the sides of the tin with zip ties, as shown. Trim off the ends with kitchen scissors.

4 Position the rubber band symmetrically on the cork as shown, so each side lies close to a craft stick. Leave even loops of rubber band on either side. Glue in place.

SPLISH!

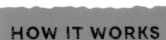

5 Slip the pencils through the rubber band loops. Wind up the rubber band by turning the propeller a few times, away from the tin.

Place in the water and release!

HOW IT WORKS

When the boat is released, the rubber band unwinds, unleashing stored energy. This makes the paddle revolve and dig into the water, pulling the boat forward.

REAL-WORLD ENGINEERING

In a traditional paddle boat, a big **paddle wheel** at the rear or side of the boat rotates like a tire and pushes water straight back, so the boat goes forward. A steam engine rotates the wheel, which can move forward or backward.

WATER BUG

It's fun to watch water bugs whizzing about on water as if by magic. Now you can make your own cool, motorized version that only moves when you want it to!

TOOLS:

- Craft knife
- Tape measure
- Wire cutters
- Needle-nose pliers
- Gaffer tape (or duct tape)
- Hot glue gun or Epoxy glue
- Clear tape

YOU WILL NEED:

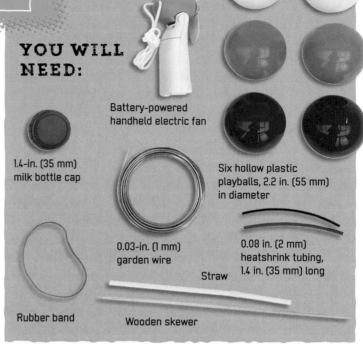

Battery-powered handheld electric fan

1.4-in. (35 mm) milk bottle cap

Six hollow plastic playballs, 2.2 in. (55 mm) in diameter

0.03-in. (1 mm) garden wire

0.08 in. (2 mm) heatshrink tubing, 1.4 in. (35 mm) long

Straw

Rubber band

Wooden skewer

1 Cut out the disc of the milk bottle cap with a utility knife. Draw a three-lobed shape for the propeller. Cut it out. Make a small hole in the center that will fit the wooden skewer tightly.

2 Use pliers to make up a 12-in. (300 mm) length of wire into the shape as shown. The sides of the U should match the length of the fan, about 2.2 in (55 mm). Tape the straight end to the straw with gaffer tape.

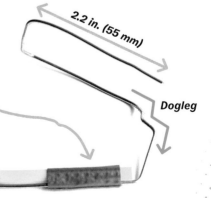

2.2 in. (55 mm)

Dogleg

3 Pull the fan head off the fan to reveal the motor shaft. Join the skewer to the shaft with the heatshrink tubing.

4 Cut off the bendy bit of straw and thread the skewer all the way through the straight section. Tape the looped end of the wire to the fan with gaffer tape. Glue the propeller to the end of the skewer with a hot glue gun or Epoxy.

5 Use wire cutters to cut three 28-in. (700 mm) lengths of wire and bend them into a narrow U-shape. Tape them together with gaffer tape just below the U-bend.

6 Separate the wires out evenly as shown, with the pair nearest the U bent back the most, the next pair in the center, and the top pair facing forward.

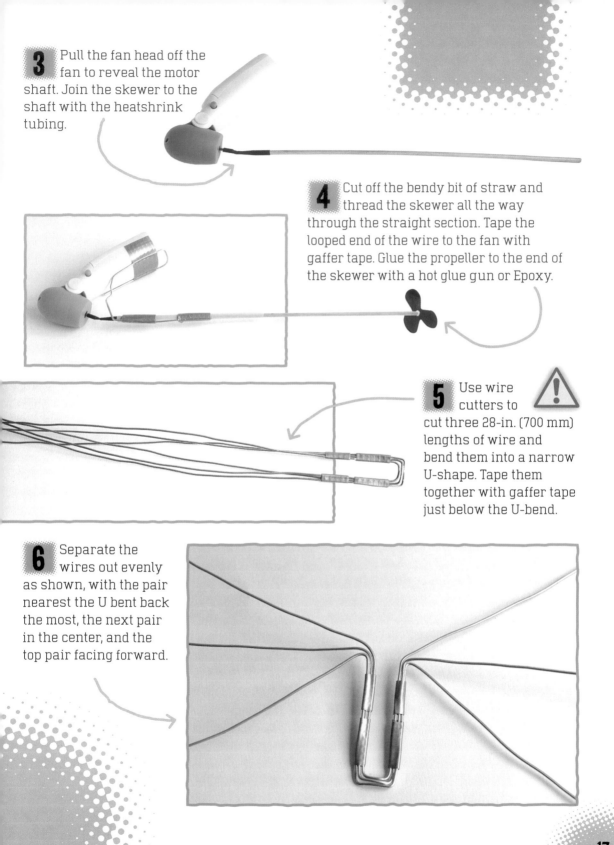

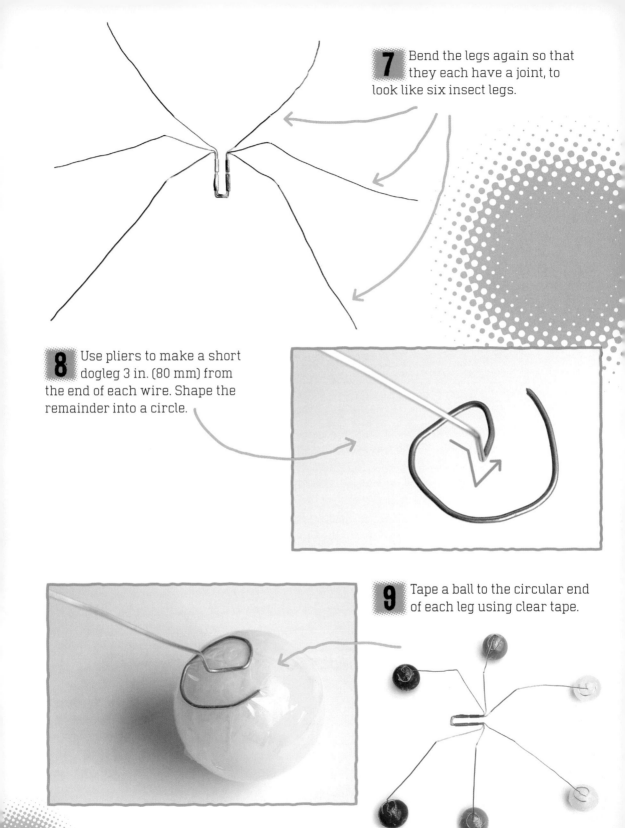

7 Bend the legs again so that they each have a joint, to look like six insect legs.

8 Use pliers to make a short dogleg 3 in. (80 mm) from the end of each wire. Shape the remainder into a circle.

9 Tape a ball to the circular end of each leg using clear tape.

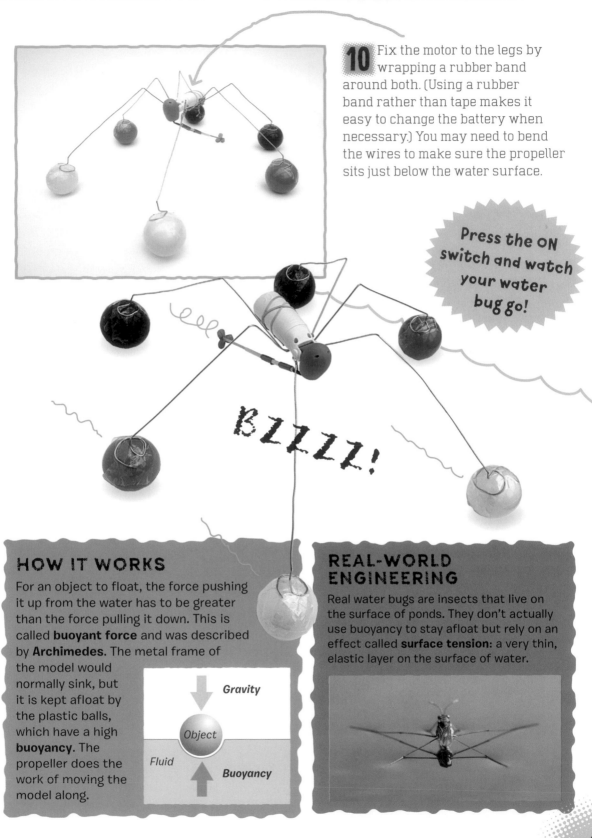

10 Fix the motor to the legs by wrapping a rubber band around both. (Using a rubber band rather than tape makes it easy to change the battery when necessary.) You may need to bend the wires to make sure the propeller sits just below the water surface.

Press the ON switch and watch your water bug go!

BZZZZ!

HOW IT WORKS

For an object to float, the force pushing it up from the water has to be greater than the force pulling it down. This is called **buoyant force** and was described by **Archimedes**. The metal frame of the model would normally sink, but it is kept afloat by the plastic balls, which have a high **buoyancy**. The propeller does the work of moving the model along.

Gravity

Object

Fluid

Buoyancy

REAL-WORLD ENGINEERING

Real water bugs are insects that live on the surface of ponds. They don't actually use buoyancy to stay afloat but rely on an effect called **surface tension:** a very thin, elastic layer on the surface of water.

SAIL AWAY

A raft is the simplest of all boats, and in early designs, logs were lashed together with rope. Copy that idea using light materials to ensure total floatability!

TOOLS:

- Craft drill
- Ruler
- Utility knife
- Kitchen scissors
- Clear tape

YOU WILL NEED:

Thin (0.2 in., or 5 mm) craft wire, 20 in. (500 mm) long

Reusable plastic shopping bag

0.6 in. (15 mm) foam pipe insulation, 60 in. (152 cm) long

Four skewers

Wooden chopstick

1 Drill a hole in the end of the chopstick with a craft drill to fit a skewer. Cut five 12-in. (300 mm) lengths of pipe insulation with a utility knife.

2 Push the drilled end of the chopstick into the center of one tube so it sits inside. Thread a skewer along the tube and through the hole in the chopstick. This will hold the chopstick upright.

3 Line up the remaining four foam tubes and thread a skewer through the sides, about 1.6 in. (40 mm) from either end, to join them together.

4 Cut out a sail, 8 in. (200 mm) square, from the plastic bag. Make a notch in the middle of the top edge, 1 in. (30 mm) deep.

You're ready to sail the ocean blue!

5 Fold this edge over a skewer and tape it down. Tie the center of the skewer to the top of the chopstick with craft wire.

6 Attach the bottom corners of the sail to the ends of the back skewer with craft wire. Trim off excess wire and the skewer ends with scissors.

HOW IT WORKS

The raft uses a buoyant material, and its regular shape disperses weight evenly to keep it stable. The sail allows it to skim along with the wind!

REAL-WORLD ENGINEERING

Wind is moving air and is caused by differences in **air pressure**. Air under high pressure will move to areas of low pressure. The bigger the difference, the faster it flows and the stronger the wind. A square sail will "catch the wind" but can only carry a boat in the wind's direction. A triangular sail can move across the wind to take you where you want to go!

DEEP DIVER

Imagine how strange it must feel to dive to the depths of the ocean in a submarine! Get a similar sinking feeling with a carefully constructed bottle sub, complete with a propeller and hydroplanes. You're the COB (Chief of the Boat) and are in control of its "bubble" (up or down angle).

TOOLS:
- Craft drill
- Tape measure
- Utility knife
- Needle-nose pliers
- Wire cutters
- Scissors

YOU WILL NEED:

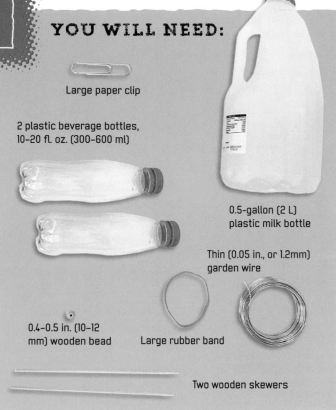

Large paper clip

2 plastic beverage bottles, 10–20 fl. oz. (300–600 ml)

0.5-gallon (2 L) plastic milk bottle

Thin (0.05 in., or 1.2mm) garden wire

0.4–0.5 in. (10–12 mm) wooden bead

Large rubber band

Two wooden skewers

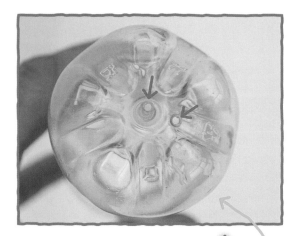

1 Drill two holes in the bottom of one of the plastic bottles, one in the center and one 0.4 in. (10 mm) off-center.

2 Drill a hole in the center of the bottle lid.

3 Use a utility knife to cut out a five-blade propeller shape from the base of the other plastic bottle.

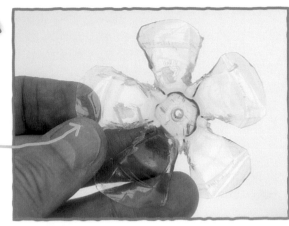

4 Use pliers to straighten out the paper clip. Make a hook at one end and loop the rubber band over. Thread the other end through the hole in the lid, the bead, and the propeller. Secure the wire by twisting it and fit the lid on the bottle.

5 Make a hook in the end of a 16-in. (400 mm) length of wire and push it through the center hole in the bottom of the bottle. Hook it over the rubber band and pull it into the bottle to about 1 in. (25 mm) from the bottom.

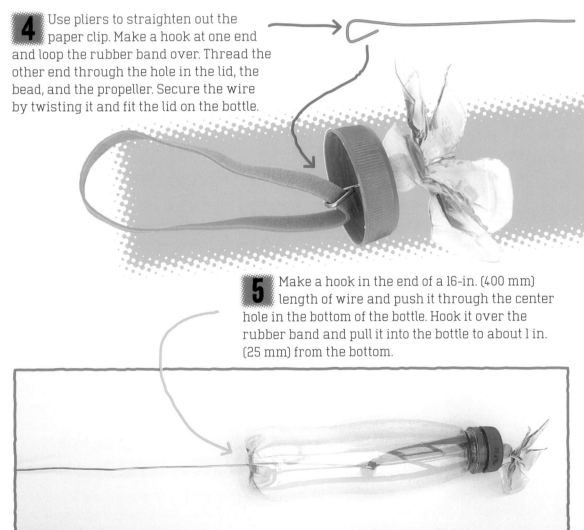

6 Use the pliers to bend the wire into a loop as shown and cut off any excess with wire cutters. Push the free end of the wire into the off-center hole to secure it.

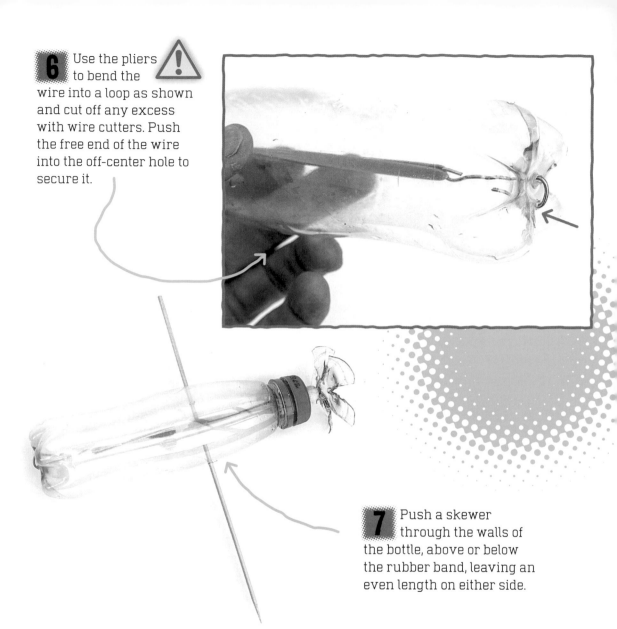

7 Push a skewer through the walls of the bottle, above or below the rubber band, leaving an even length on either side.

HOW IT WORKS

Since the bottle is light and has high buoyancy, it needs water to weigh it down and take it below the surface. You can decide how much to add according to how far it sinks and how far you want it to sink! The propeller does exactly the same thin as a real sub's propellers, only it rotates by rubber band power rather than by electric motor.

CROSS SECTION OF A SUBMARINE

Outer hull mainly filled with air: sub rises

Outer hull filled with water: sub sinks

Outer hull partly filled with water: sub hovers

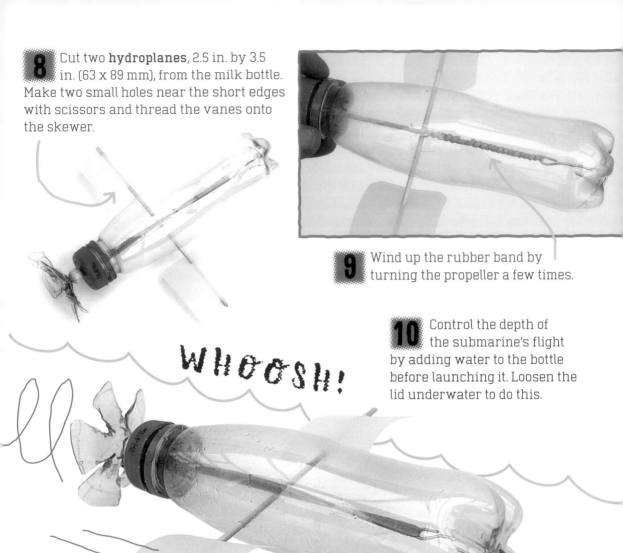

8 Cut two **hydroplanes**, 2.5 in. by 3.5 in. (63 x 89 mm), from the milk bottle. Make two small holes near the short edges with scissors and thread the vanes onto the skewer.

9 Wind up the rubber band by turning the propeller a few times.

10 Control the depth of the submarine's flight by adding water to the bottle before launching it. Loosen the lid underwater to do this.

WHOOSH!

REAL-WORLD ENGINEERING

Submarines use ballast tanks to control their buoyancy. As the tanks are filled with water, the submarine sinks deeper. When water in the tanks is emptied, the submarine floats back to the surface. Hydroplanes on the side of the sub are also used to move it up and down, like the wings on an airplane.

SWAMP BOAT

Want to explore the Florida Everglades or the mangrove forests of Malaysia? What you need is a swamp boat! With this clever craft, you'll never get tangled up in all that low-growing greenery.

YOU WILL NEED:

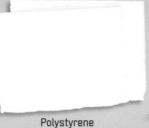

Polystyrene scraps

Craft foam sheets

Two skewers

Corrugated cardboard scraps

3V electric motor

Craft cork (not plastic)

Large paper clip

Two zip ties

3V battery holder with switch

... and two ballpoint pens

TOOLS:

- Utility knife
- Tracing paper and pencil
- Super glue
- Craft drill
- Ruler
- Scissors
- Hot glue gun

1 Cut a cork in half lengthwise with a utility knife. Cut a slot on each side of one half, so that they're angled in opposite directions.

2 Use this template (actual size) to trace and cut two blades from craft foam. Fit them into the slots in the cork and secure them with a dot of super glue.

BLADE template

2.4 inches (60 mm)

1 inch (27 mm)

3 Drill a small hole in the center of the cork to fit tightly over the motor.

4 Fit two batteries into the battery holder.

5 Wire up the motor to the batteries, red to the positive terminal and black to the negative terminal.

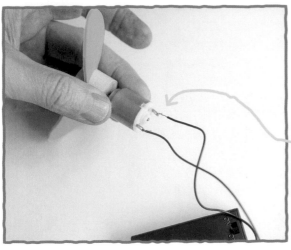

6 Use a zip tie to join the motor and battery holder together to make a power unit. Trim the end of the tie with scissors.

7 Use model below (not actual size) to create a template to trace out a hull and **bow** (front). Cut two hulls and one bow from polystyrene with a utility knife. Glue the hulls together with a hot glue gun, then glue on the bow.

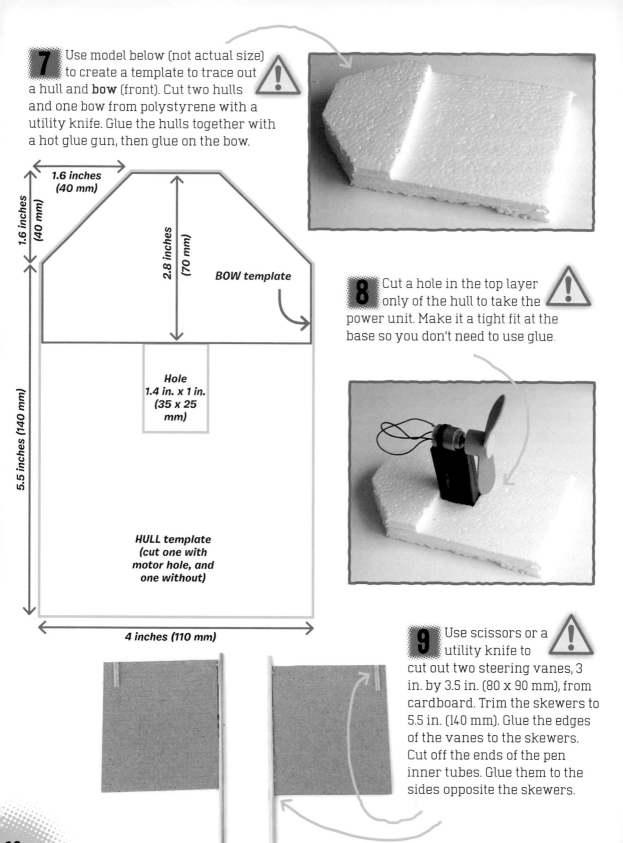

1.6 inches (40 mm)

1.6 inches (40 mm)

2.8 inches (70 mm)

BOW template

Hole 1.4 in. x 1 in. (35 x 25 mm)

5.5 inches (140 mm)

HULL template (cut one with motor hole, and one without)

4 inches (110 mm)

8 Cut a hole in the top layer only of the hull to take the power unit. Make it a tight fit at the base so you don't need to use glue.

9 Use scissors or a utility knife to cut out two steering vanes, 3 in. by 3.5 in. (80 x 90 mm), from cardboard. Trim the skewers to 5.5 in. (140 mm). Glue the edges of the vanes to the skewers. Cut off the ends of the pen inner tubes. Glue them to the sides opposite the skewers.

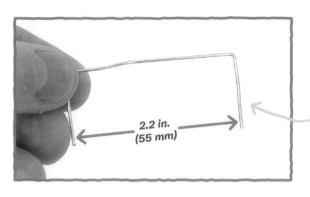

10 Use pliers to straighten out the paper clip and shape it as shown.

2.2 in. (55 mm)

11 Fit the vanes to the back of the boat, 0.6 in. (15 mm) from the sides. Join them together by slotting the ends of the paper clip into the pen inner tubes.

Launch your boat in a swamp, switch on the motor, and dodge the crocs!

VSSSHHH!

HOW IT WORKS

You can try out your boat on a weedy pond and see why its flat bottom is so practical—it won't get stuck in the weeds. For the same reason, the propeller is on the deck rather than submerged, as in other boats—so the swamp boat's operating parts can work freely. The boat is steered by pushing the vanes in the direction you want.

REAL-WORLD ENGINEERING

Real swamp boats are made from very buoyant materials so that they float high in the water. They have a shallow draft and are moved by a big propeller that creates a column of air pushing backward. The operator makes the air column move left or right with a stick and sits high up to get a good view of obstacles ahead.

GLOSSARY

AIR PRESSURE
The weight of air at any given point. Air pressure depends on the air's density, or how close together the molecules are. Warm air is less dense and creates less pressure, so it rises. Cold air is denser and creates more pressure.

AIR PROPELLER
A shaft mounted with two or more blades and powered by an engine to rotate and provide the force needed for lift and movement. The pitch, or angle, of the blades may be varied according to the required speed and air resistance. The word comes from the Latin *pellere*, meaning to push or drive.

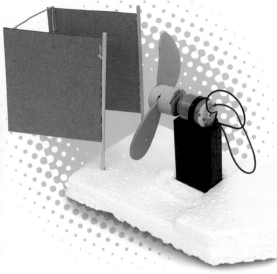

ARCHIMEDES
Mathematician and engineer of ancient Greece, famous for working out the law of buoyancy (*see below*), also called Archimedes' principle. It's said that he figured this out while lying in his bath! He is the founder of hydrostatics, the study of fluids, and is credited with inventing the Archimedes screw. This is a machine for moving water from a lower to a higher level.

BUOYANCY, BUOYANT FORCE
The upward force exerted on an object fully or partly submerged in a liquid (or gas), also known as Archimedes' principle. The buoyant force is equal in magnitude to the weight of the fluid displaced by the object. For example, a ship sinks into the sea until the amount of water it displaces (pushes aside) equals its own weight. A heavier ship will displace more water and be kept afloat by the equivalent buoyant force.

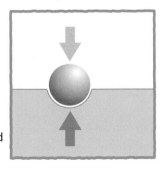

DRAFT
The distance between the surface of water and the lowest point on a vessel's hull. This varies widely in watercraft, depending on what they are built to do. A shallow draft vessel is needed for shallow water and where there are submerged plants or objects. A deep draft vessel is able to carry heavy loads and remain stable in the water.

HULL

The lower part of a ship that floats in the water. There are different shapes of hull—flat, rounded, or V-shaped—and the lowest part is the keel, which runs like a backbone along the center.

HYDROPLANE

A flap on the side of a submarine that helps it to submerge. It acts like a wing but works in water, not air. There is usually a pair fitted on either side of the bow and stern (front and back), which allows the sub to be angled up or down.

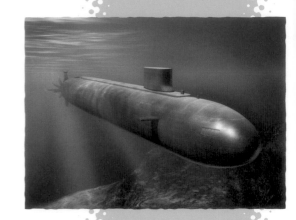

PADDLE WHEEL

A large steel-frame wheel, fitted on the outside with evenly spaced paddle blades. It is rotated by an engine to provide thrust, and the lowest quarter is always underwater. The Romans used a type of paddle boat, and it was the main means of transport on calm bodies of water such as lakes and wide rivers of the United States throughout the nineteenth century.

BOW

The pointed front of a boat or ship, also known as the prow.

SURFACE TENSION

The elastic effect at the surface of water created by the way the water molecules are attracted to each other.

THRUST

The powerful force produced by a machine in one direction that gives it an equally strong movement in the opposite direction. In a space rocket, for example, burning fuel creates a mass of gases under pressure. The gases have to go somewhere, so they blast out the back with a force strong enough to propel the craft up and away from Earth.

INDEX

air propeller, 9
Archimedes, 19

ballast tanks, 25
buoyancy, 19, 24–25, 29
buoyant force, 19

catamaran, 8–9

fish, 10–11

jet boat, 12–13

Newton's Third Law of
    Motion, 9

paddle boat, 14–15

raft, 20–21

submarine, 22–25
surface tension, 19
swamp boat, 26–29

thrust, 13

vortex, 11

water bug, 16–19

THE AUTHOR

Rob Ives is a former math and science teacher, currently a designer and paper engineer living in Cumbria, UK. He creates science- and project-based children's books, including *Paper Models that Rock!* and *Paper Automata*. He specializes in character-based paper animations and all kinds of fun and fascinating science projects, and he often visits schools to talk about design technology and to demonstrate his models. Rob's other series for Hungry Tomato include *Tabletop Battles* and *Amazing Science Experiments*.

Picture Credits
(abbreviations: t = top; b = bottom;
c = center; l = left; r = right)
Shutterstock.com: Alessandro De
Maddalena 11br; Andrea Danti 25br & 31tr;
Claudio Gennari 6tr & 9br; gibleho 15br;
holbox 29br & 30bl; PRILL 31bl; sainthorant
daniel 21br; Zadiraka Evgenii 19br.

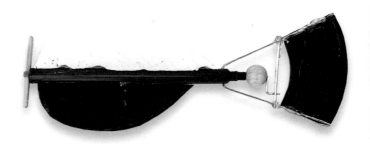